WISDOM

God's Golden Key To Success

MIKE MURDOCK

Unless otherwise indicated, all Scripture quotations are taken from the King James Version of the Bible.

Wisdom—God's Golden Key to Success
Wisdom Key Books
ISBN 1-56-394-039-6
Copyright © 1995 by Mike Murdock
P.O. Box 99
Dallas, Texas 75221

Published by
Wisdom International
P.O. Box 747
Dallas, Texas 75221

Printed in the United States of America.

Wisdom—God's Golden Key to Success

God wants you successful! Are you shocked by this statement? Thousands of people throughout the world are experiencing a revolution in their lives. Spiritual rebirth, physical healings, financial miracles are happening to people *just like you!* People are seeing what God is *really* like, and this photograph is igniting a fire of excitement like they have never experienced before.

Everything God can do was meant to happen to *you!*

1

Three Important Keys About You!

Key #1
You Have Worth.

Everything God creates has tremendous value. This makes you the object of God's attention and affection. Your life can be changed just by understanding these explosive truths.

Key #2
God Created You.

He made you in His image, after His form and likeness. The Bible teaches that you and I are God's highest creation. Man is given dominion over everything else God made, over the earth and all its inhabitants.

Key #3
God Placed At Your Disposal An Unlimited Wealth Of Resources.

As the Owner of everything in the universe, God intended that His people should not lack for anything. And He intended that man should know how to make full use of every resource. So He implanted within you the "seeds for success" in every area of your life. As His supreme creation, God poured into you His mind, His power, His sensitivity, His Wisdom—everything necessary for you to succeed.

Your success is always on God's mind. Very early in the Word of God it is established that success and prosperity are worthy and worthwhile goals for man in God's eyes. In Joshua 1:7-8 we read: "Only be thou strong and very courageous, that thou mayest observe to do according to all the law, which Moses my servant commanded thee: turn not from it to the right hand or to the left, that thou mayest prosper whithersoever thou goest. This book of the law shall not depart out of thy mouth; but thou shalt *meditate* therein *day and night,* that thou mayest observe to do according to all that is written therein: for then *thou shalt make thy way prosperous,* and then thou shalt have good success."

These verses are highly significant. They establish in no uncertain terms that God wants you *successful* and to enjoy *prosperity.* God's will is that "thou mayest prosper withersoever thou goest." As you follow His divine formulas for success taught in the Word of God, "then thou shalt make thy way prosperous, and then thou shalt have good success."

There is no mistaking what the Bible says. Either you believe the Word of God, or you don't. If you accept the Bible as being true, then you must believe God wants His children to be successful. Three reasons why God delights in your total success stand out.

2

Three Reasons God Wants You to Succeed

Reason # 1
Your Life Is On Display.

God wants your success to serve as an example of what His love and power can do in a person's life. By sending success into the lives of His children, God can demonstrate to an unbelieving world both His *nature* and His *power.* The Apostle Paul wrote: *"But God hath chosen the foolish things of the world to confound the wise; and God hath chosen the weak things of the world to confound the things which are mighty;"* (I Corinthians 1:27). He also testified that God dealt with him and said: *". . . my strength is made perfect in weakness. . ."* (II Corinthians 12:9).

Have you ever known people who seemed to be the model of success in every area of life—spiritually, physically, and mentally? Their life appeared almost perfect. Their financial condition was stable. Their family and social life was an example of all that is wholesome, healthy and desirable.

Yet, as you studied those individuals, you found it hard to pinpoint the *secret* of their success. Do you know what I mean? There seemed to be no outstanding abilities or resources within these people for them to draw from. Maybe you have looked at people like this and wondered what their real secret was.

The real key to any truly successful life is *daily* obedience.

For instance, Abraham's obedience brought the blessings of God in abundance. He served as an example to each of us what God wants for His children. *"And if ye be Christ's, then are ye Abraham's seed, and heirs according to the promise"* (Galatians 3:29).

Reason #2
To Provide For Your Family.

God wants to give you success to enable you to provide for your family needs. The Bible makes it explicitly clear that we must provide for the material as well as for the spiritual needs of our families, if we are to be successful spiritual leaders: *"But if any provide not for his own, and specially for those of his own house, he hath denied the faith, and is worse than an infidel"* (I Timothy 5:8).

God gets no glory if your family has to live in a rat-breeding, roach-infested tenement. He is not pleased if your family never has enough to eat, and your children wear "hand-me-downs" and go without shoes. He is a God of abundance of blessings. He wants you and your family to have plenty . . . and to spare.

Reason #3
To Carry Out The Great Commission.

God wants you successful to financially support and undergird the work of God. As God sends prosperity into your life, He not only meets your needs, but also makes it possible for you to help carry out *the Great Commission.* Someone has said that money in the hands of an unbeliever is a snare, but money in the hands of a believer is a *tool* to do God's will.

As Christians are prospered financially and use their resources for God's work, *good things start happening.* Churches are built, mission stations are established, gospel radio and television programs are aired and soul winning ministries are launched to share the message of salvation with those who have not yet been born again. All these things cost money. Therefore, God prospers His people so there will be no shortage of funds to do His work.

Thousands of people have misunderstood God's attitude toward success and prosperity. Somewhere they have gotten the idea that it is wrong to want to be successful. In fact, some even feel that prosperity is of the devil. *Nothing could be further from the truth!* Don't be misled. God does want you successful! His Word does say: *". . . thou shalt make thy way prosperous, and then thou shalt have good success"* (Joshua 1:8).

Money In The Hand Of An Unbeliever Is Often A Snare But, In The Hand Of A Child Of God, It Can Be An Effective Tool To Carry Out The Great Commission.

3

What Is Success?

When you say the word success, everybody thinks of yachts, gorgeous homes, big cars, fancy clothes, and big bank accounts. It is quite possible to have all these possessions and be successful. Unfortunately, merely having these possessions does not necessarily make a person successful. Many who possess all of this have honestly admitted openly that they are still unhappy with their life.

Some people define success in terms of power, position, prestige and popularity. Again, the successful person may enjoy all these things. But even these attributes are not in themselves the foundation stones of success.

Still others say that success is *achieving the goals* you set for yourself. The question is, does the attainment of those particular goals produce *genuine satisfaction* in the heart, the inner world? The external picture of success does not necessarily guarantee *internal* happiness.

I remember reading in history about Alexander the Great. He went out with his armies to conquer the nations of the world. After the last victorious battle had ended, it is said Alexander wept because there were no more worlds left for him to conquer! He achieved *all* his goals but did *not* find abiding satisfaction and happiness.

4

Real Success

If success is not measured in terms of possessions, popularity or performance, how then can it be defined? Perhaps the simplest definition of success for the believer is knowing and attaining God's goals for your life. *A successful life is one that is happy.*

Becoming what God wants you to become.

Doing what God wants you to do.

Possessing what God wants you to own.

As you achieve the goals *God* has set for your life, *then* you become successful. Someone once said, "Success is not merely getting what you want, but *wanting what you got after you get it.*" Some fellow may throw away all he has to win the heart of a certain girl, only to discover later her greatest talent is making him miserable! *He got what he wanted, but didn't want what he got.*

In their quest for achievement, some people become so greedy and grasping they are never satisfied with any accomplishment. They never enjoy what God has *already* given them.

Real success is not a destination, it is a journey. It is *movement.* It is the joy created by *progress.* Success is not a city where you will arrive *tomorrow*, it is the enjoyment of today, the *now*. Every person is somewhere on God's maturity schedule, from "A" to "Z." Real success is keeping the schedule God has for you and *His assignment for your life.*

5

Stay On God's Schedule for Success

What does all this mean? Simply that *success means different things to different people*, depending on where they are on God's maturity schedule. If someone offered a baby the keys to a new car, it would mean very little to him. He wants his bottle of milk! Having the keys to his own automobile would not be success to him. Being given his bottle and a soft pillow for his head is the best thing that could happen to him right now.

However, if that baby continued to progress along God's maturity schedule, about 16 years later, if he were offered a baby bottle and a soft pillow, he would be very disappointed. It would not be his idea of the ideal way to spend an evening. That's the time he is interested in the offer of the keys to the car!

That's why I say *true success is achieving the goals God presently has for you*. Some Christians have stopped along God's maturity schedule at about letter "C." Instead of realizing God wants them to prosper and be successful, they sit back with a "baby bottle" and wonder why they find very little satisfaction in life.

On the other hand, it is possible to try to get *too far ahead of God's schedule.* I know some people who are trying to achieve level "S" or "T" when they should be back on about "M." Because of their misdirected attention focus, they are completely dissatisfied with the achievements they are making on their present level.

Remember, *success is different things to different people at different times.* Find out where you are on your journey. Learn to enjoy what you are already receiving instead of being unhappy because you haven't got everything you are wanting.

One man I know thought his "success goal" was a lot of money. You can imagine how he felt when he read in the newspaper about a guy who won a contest and was awarded the prize of $100,000. "Wow, what a lucky guy," the man said. "Nothing could make me unhappy if I could win $100,000 like he did!"

Then my friend read the next paragraph of the news story. He learned that the "winner" was a prisoner on death row, scheduled to be electrocuted in a short time. From the prisoner's point of view, the $100,000 prize didn't spell success. The money wasn't going to do him much good!

Never forget that being successful is achieving the goals *God* has for you in *every area* of your life. What are these areas? God has a success plan for you spiritually, physically, emotionally, financially, socially and in your family life. And He has provided *a golden key* to help you *unlock* the doors of success in every single area.

Success is the achievement of the goals God has for you!

6

God's Golden Key

When I was growing up, all the kids in the neighborhood would gather around to talk. One of our favorite topics was the "one-wish game." Someone would say, "If you could have anything in the whole world, what one thing would you wish for?"

The girls usually wanted a date with some popular guy at school. The fellow down the block wished for a motorcycle. A teenager who was having problems at home might say he wished he had no parents! One girl wished she had $1,000 to spend on new clothes.

Everyone in the group always had one or two things to wish for. Every time we played the game there always was something each youngster either wanted to have or wished to avoid. Of course, there was no one listening to our wishes who had the power to grant them. One day a new boy in our neighborhood stunned us all by his statement of his one wish, "I wish for one thing—the wishing ability that anything I wish for would come true." Naturally, for such clever thinking he became our leading local genius!

There is a story in the Bible, though, of a man who was actually guaranteed that he would be given anything he asked for: *". . .the LORD appeared to Solomon in a dream by night: and God said, Ask what I shall give thee"* (I Kings 3:5).

What a dramatic situation! It was as if God had led Solomon to the front of a great hotel and said, "Choose any room you want, and you can have it. One room has riches inside. Another has long life. One room has power and authority. Each room contains something desirable—something you would like to have. Just tell me which room you want most and *I will give you the key to it.*"

Solomon thought about God's offer for a moment. Then he said quietly, "Give me the key to the room which contains *Wisdom* and understanding."

God smiled, and opened up the ring of keys in His hand. He took off a golden key and handed it to Solomon. "You have made a wise choice," He said.

Solomon asked, "Why is this key different from the rest?"

"Because this is the *master key*—it will unlock *all* the rooms in the entire building!"

Yes, *Wisdom is God's golden key to your success.* Wisdom! At first it sounds like nothing. It seems trite and meaningless. But Wisdom is the master key that opens the doors of opportunity to you and gives you free access to every resource. Wisdom *unlocks the doors* to all your goals, ambitions, and desires. Wisdom will *smash the locks* on your prison of prejudices, fears and unhappiness!

7

What Is Wisdom?

Wisdom is the sum total of *both* knowledge and under-standing. *It is the ability to interpret life as God sees it*—the ability to see the total picture that God sees of a person or a situation. Wisdom is the ability:

- To *see* through His eyes,

- To *hear* through His ears,

- To *feel* as with His heart,

- To *walk* in His steps,

- To *think* with His mind.

No marriage would ever be destroyed by divorce if the husband saw his wife through the eyes of God, and the wife could see her husband as God sees him.

A man would be able to become wealthy almost overnight *if he knew the hearts of people* and all the details of business propositions as God knows them.

Parents and children would have no crushing conflicts if they dealt with each other from the standpoint of wisdom. How many teenagers look at their parents and wish they could go pack their bags and leave home because nobody understands them? While they are thinking that, the parents' hearts are just aching: "Oh honey, if you could just see how we love you. If you could just know how we think and feel about you!"

The golden key of Wisdom makes it possible for parents and children to *communicate*—to hear what the other is saying with his heart. Understanding will open the door to harmony and happiness in the home.

Wisdom is also *seeing God's purpose in some of life's more unpleasant events.* The Bible tells how Joseph was sold into slavery by his brothers. As a slave, he tried to do what was right and was the target of vicious lies as a result. He ended up in a dungeon. Through all this pain and persecution, Joseph maintained his faith in God. How? By being aware of God's hand at work in his behalf. Because he was in the dungeon at the right time, he was given the opportunity to minister by interpreting Pharaoh's troubling dreams. This catapulted him to power. In a short time he had become Pharaoh's chief officer of the entire land. With God's direction he was able to prepare for a time of great famine in the land.

When the famine came, Joseph was able to save an entire nation. Plus, he was in a position to save the lives of his own family—including the brothers who had betrayed him. Wisdom helped him to *see God's purpose in his problems* and make him successful.

By using the golden key of Wisdom, we can unlock the doors of *opportunity* in every part of our lives, even in our

---

Pain Is Often A Bridge, Not A Barricade, To Success.

---

finances, and walk through them confidently, to gain success. When you ask God for the Golden Key of Wisdom, He says to you: *"...I am the LORD thy God which teacheth thee to profit, which leadeth thee by the way that thou shouldest go"* (Isaiah 48:17).

8

$124,000 Profit in 30 Days!

A friend of mine was driving by a piece of property, and suddenly he felt a strong impression that he should buy it. The selling price was $75,000, and my friend didn't have that kind of money. He couldn't see why he should buy such an expensive piece of ground that he didn't even need. But the voice of God kept speaking to him. *God knew something he didn't know and wanted to share it with him.*

My friend felt this leading of the Lord so strongly that he began scraping together what money he could. He took all of his savings out of the bank. He sold some items. He took all the cash he could get together and made a down payment on that piece of property.

Thirty days later he was on that lot, burning some trash and generally cleaning up a bit. A car drove up and a lady got out, walked over and asked if he was the owner. Then she wanted to know if the property was for sale.

When my friend assured her he was the owner, she said, "My husband is a doctor. He has been wanting to buy this land for four years. We're prepared to offer you $199,000 for this property."

In 30 days time, my friend was offered a $124,000 profit! He was able to achieve this remarkable success—not in his own wisdom, but through the divine Wisdom of God— the ability to see the picture of that property *as God saw it.* His obedience created the miracle.

What God did for this man, *He will do for you.* God is no respecter of persons. His promises are for *everybody.* He has a Golden Key of Wisdom *waiting for you!*

You Create A Season Of Success Every Time You Complete An Instruction From God.

9

Where Does Wisdom Come From?

*A*ll *Wisdom comes from God.* It is a gift only God can give. That is why Solomon had to ask for Wisdom instead of trying to rely upon himself. God bestows understanding upon us through His Word: *"For the LORD giveth wisdom: out of his mouth cometh knowledge and understanding"* (Proverbs 2:6). The Psalmist said of God: *"Through thy precepts I get understanding:"* (Psalms 119:104).

So the Word of God opens up Wisdom to us. The entire Bible was written that you and I would have *Wisdom*—that we would be able to interpret life as God does. Paul, one of the most prolific writers of the New Testament, said: *"Consider what I say; and the Lord give thee understanding in all things"* (II Timothy 2:7).

By carefully reading the Word of God, we *learn* to use the Golden Key of Wisdom to unlock the doors of success. As we immerse ourselves in the *Bible*, God speaks to us from His Word and says, "This is what I *think*. This is what I know. This is what I *see*. This is what I *hear*."

God has breathed His divine knowledge into the Word. *Between the covers of your Bible are the treasures you need to be truly successful.* You will find the answer to financial troubles, how to cure worry, even how to solve friendship problems. The Word will direct you in your family relationships—the chain of authority in the home, including the position of the husband, the wife, and the children. The Bible contains a cure for nervousness and depression. The Word is even the purging tool for removing immorality from our minds and lives: *"Wherewithal shall a young man cleanse his way? by taking heed thereto according to thy word"* (Psalms 119:9).

So, the Bible is the *Success Book* of the world! It is the source of God's golden key for success: *"The entrance of thy words giveth light; it giveth understanding unto the simple"* (Psalms 119:130).

An interesting note is that one of the most important functions of the Holy Spirit is to *interpret* the Word of God to believers and *produce* Wisdom. This means when we come across a passage of Scripture that is not clear to us, the Holy Spirit enlightens our minds and makes every detail sharp and meaningful: *"Howbeit when he, the Spirit of truth, is come, he will guide you into all truth:"* (John 16:13a). It was this Spirit that rested upon Jesus as Isaiah prophesied: *"And the spirit of the LORD shall rest upon him, the spirit of wisdom and understanding"* (Isaiah 11:2a). But we must desire and *ask* for this Wisdom. If we will do that, God will give it to us liberally according to James 1:5: *"If any of you lack wisdom, let him ask of God, that giveth to all men liberally, and upbraideth not; and it shall be given him."*

10

Your Study Program for Success

Your *regularity* in Bible study is vitally important. It helps unfold God's total requirements for success through enlightenment and Wisdom. As you delve into the rich Wisdom of the Bible, you will come to understand God, others and yourself.

1. As you learn the truth about *God* and find out about His nature, His opinions, and His sense of values, you experience the thrill of discovering where He wants you, when He wants you there, and how He chooses to place you there.

2. The Bible enables you to see *others* as God sees them. You begin to understand their place in your life. And you learn to recognize and *anticipate their needs* and the part God wants you to have in ministering to them.

3. God's Word helps you come to a better understanding of *yourself.* You begin to catch a glimpse of the importance God places on you. You start to interpret yourself as

God sees you, both now and potentially. You will see more than your problems. You will begin to see the *possibilities* God sees in you.

To receive God's golden key—Wisdom—establish regular Bible study habits. Start *consuming* the Word of God. *The best advice I can offer you is to set a definite daily study time.* Spend part of that time just reading—not trying to delve deeply into complex theological concepts. Simply read what God has to say, and let the Word speak to your heart.

Maybe you would enjoy selecting one subject that appeals to you to study further and become an expert on that specific topic. Perhaps you are interested in angels, or healing, or prophecy. *Begin to become a Bible expert on that particular subject.* Bible helps, concordances, commentaries and other research material will enable you to find everything the Bible has to say and to compare opinions of other scholars about the subject you have chosen. This will give you confidence in your knowledge of the Word. Also, be sure the Bible you use has easy-to-read type of a comfortable size.

11

Learning the Way of the Winner

Keep in mind always that the Bible is a *Book of Success*. It tells you about people's successes and failures. It is literally the book that shows you the "Way of the Winner."

The Word of God outlines how you can be a *victor* instead of a *victim*—how you can win instead of losing. It teaches you to have a *sonship mentality* instead of a *slave mentality*.

The Bible tells you *how to think*. It shows what influences you. It outlines everything you need to know about God, everything you need to know about yourself, and everything you need to know about people and their behavior.

Last, but certainly not least, the Word of God can make you happy. One of the side benefits of success is happiness. The Bible says: *"Happy is the man that findeth wisdom, and the man that getteth understanding"* (Proverbs 3:13).

So now you know where Wisdom comes from, and how to go about finding success and happiness through the Word of God. *Don't let anything stop you from using this key* to open up a whole new world for yourself. Satan will try to divert you, distract you, interrupt you—anything to keep you from finding the success he knows the Bible will open up for you. But keep to your purpose. As the Word begins to come alive in you, your desire and appetite for the Bible will increase. Then you will be well on your way to *habitual* victory.

God's Word Is The Key To Success And Happiness.
Use This Key Every Day!

12

Develop a New Picture of Yourself

T*he Bible is the original book of success.* It is a Book of *Pictures.* It gives you a picture of *God.* It gives you a picture of *yourself.* It gives you a picture of *others.* In the Bible you can see a picture of Abraham and his success. You can see a picture of Joseph and his success. You can even see pictures of people like Elijah, Jonah, and Paul in moments of stress, as well as in moments of triumph. As you become more and more familiar with the Word of God, you build into the gallery of your mind a collection of photographs of the success stories of the Bible.

As you study these pictures, you will soon discover *another* image beginning to take shape. You will recognize this as a picture of *you.* You begin to see yourself, not as what you have been, but as what you are going to be. You see yourself, not where you have been, but *where you are going.* You see a picture, not of what you have done, but of what you are going to do. This fresh mental picture of yourself should become your goal. Through daily Scripture intake, you can *reinforce that picture of yourself,* as God sees you.

Your own destiny can be determined by the way *you see yourself.* Never permit yourself to say, "I'm stupid. I'm dumb. I'm a failure."

Instead, see yourself as mentally sharp, brilliant, a winner. Why? Because you have access to the mind of God. The Bible says: *"Let this mind be in you, which was also in Christ Jesus: Who, being in the form of God, thought it not robbery to be equal with God"* (Philippians 2:5-6).

13

Your Self–Portrait

When you see yourself with the mind of Christ, you see a *portrait of success*—a picture that has been retouched to take out the blemishes of failure and the wrinkles of weakness. What remains is the perfect likeness of a winner—and that is the way God sees you. He has a marvelous and thrilling photograph album of you. He sees all your high points, good qualities, and positive attributes.

Satan will try to show you a photograph of yourself at your worst. He tries to remind you of what you were like at your weakest point. He takes a photograph of you when you were down and out, and that is what he holds in front of your face all the time. He even puts a magnifying glass in front of the defects and says, "Look how bad you look ... how ugly you are!" *His whole purpose is to give you a different image of yourself than what God sees in you.*

So many people spend all their time looking at failure photographs of themselves and trying to cover up what is really a distorted picture. Problems between people sometimes start when we start exchanging these ugly photographs of each other. A wife looks at her husband and says, "I can't stand how disorganized you are, leaving your clothes on the floor. I'm tired of picking up after you."

He replies, "Well, look at how lazy you are. You never keep the dishes washed. You have not cooked in a week! I'm tired of coming home to a dirty house!"

People go around trading photographs of one another at their worst. . .instead of talking about the good pictures, the strong points. And as long as they do that, they keep right on being failures.

But the moment they begin seeing themselves *as God sees them*, 90 percent of their pressure areas and problem areas are released. This is because if they can see themselves through the eyes of God, they will start concentrating on their *potential*, not on their problems.

You Will Always Struggle Subconsciously To Become The Self-Portrait You Believe Yourself To Be.

14

The Success-Maker

J esus came to make men successful. He is the original Success-Maker. He came to upgrade men and women, and yes, even teenagers and children. God made you in His image. You are important and valuable to Him. You are an extension of His life and personality. You can be like Him. That's the way He meant for you to be.

"But what is God like?" Most of us have a very muddled, vague, hazy opinion of who God is. I heard about a mother who came upon her little boy busily drawing and coloring in his tablet. "What are you drawing, son?" she asked.

"A picture of God," he said.

"But Billy, nobody knows what God looks like," she told him.

The youngster thought about it a moment, then announced matter-of-factly: "They will when I get through." Oh, how I wish every minister of the gospel succeeded with that goal! It's so hard to explain beauty in a world that is often ugly and destructive. God is a good God.

Jesus came to show us what God is like. He said: *". . .he that hath seen me hath seen the Father. . ."* (John 14:9). His whole purpose was to make you successful and show you what you are capable of *becoming. . .of doing. . .of possessing.*

Take a look at the life of Jesus. He proved His power as a Success–Maker. He devoted His entire earthly ministry and life to helping people become more than they were and to have more than they had.

When Jesus saw people who were lonely, He spent *time* with them and had *fellowship* with them.

When Jesus saw people who were sick, He *healed* them.

When Jesus saw people who were eager to know more about God and life, He *taught* them.

When Jesus saw people who were hungry and faint, He *fed* them.

When Jesus saw people who were timid or bound by mediocrity, He *challenged* them to stand up, step out, launch out.

Jesus understood people, because He saw them through the eyes of His Father. That is *why* He could make them successful, for Wisdom is God's Golden Key to Success. Jesus understood the *needs* of the people and *met those needs* in such a way as to make them successful. The key to their success was Wisdom—developing a new picture of themselves in God's image.

The picture you develop for yourself is crucial to your success or failure. God wants you to see yourself as His highest creation. He is pouring His mind into you. He is pouring His power into you. He is pouring His sensitivity and His Wisdom into your life.

15

Overcoming the Slave Mentality

The Bible tells about the Israelites who were led out of bondage by Moses. This generation of Israelites were the descendants of people who had been slaves for 400 years. They had developed a slave mentality. They saw themselves as put down. They were totally dominated by others. They functioned best when someone told them what to do. For generations life had been made to happen for them, *so they didn't know how to make life happen.* They were not decision makers.

When these people approached the Promised Land, their leader sent 12 spies to scout out the land. Ten of them came back and said, "The inhabitants of the land are giants. We are like grasshoppers to them."

But two of the spies—Joshua and Caleb—had been able to find God's Golden Key to Success—Wisdom. They knew God was with them and would make them victorious in any battle. So they reported, "The inhabitants of the land are like grasshoppers to us. We are well able to overcome them."

Joshua and Caleb had the ability to interpret the situation *from God's vantage point.* This capability spelled the difference between success and failure, between victory and defeat, between life and death.

And this one secret can transform your life and change your world. *Look at every situation from a higher viewpoint than your own.* Draw on your increasing supply of Wisdom. Through faith, begin to see *through God's eyes.* Stop looking at the devil's picture of defeat, and concentrate on God's portrait of prosperity and success.

This is your ticket to the "promised land" of your own personal success. Begin speaking *aloud* what you desire, not what you dread. Speak your *expectations,* not your fears. As God's child, begin developing the son-ship mentality. Talk it. Think it. Accept and believe it. You are God's property, and that relationship makes all the difference in the world in what happens to you. See yourself *as God sees you*—you are His property!

The Day You Make A Decision About Life Is The Day Your World Will Change.

16

What You Make Happen for Others, God Will Make Happen for You

Some years ago something happened to me that literally changed the course of my life. It revolutionized my ministry. It transformed me. It made me a whole different person.

I was out in the garage that I had made into a make-shift office. I had been working for hours trying to catch up with some of my mail, filling orders, studying, writing and praying. I had been fasting five days. On the fifth day at 2:30 a.m., God spoke to my heart. Not aloud, but into my very spirit and innermost being. It was a simple sentence, but it struck me with the force of a sledgehammer blow. It echoed and resounded inside my head and engraved itself on the very walls of my heart. What was the message? Simply this, *"What you make happen for others, I will make happen for you."*

What you make happen for others, I will make happen for you.

I realized God was speaking to me. He burned this truth deep within my consciousness. Over and over those words came to me, and more and more I began to see this was the golden thread in the garment of life.

If I make good happen for others, God will make good happen for me. If I cause bad things to happen to others, bad things will happen to me. It works both ways. And it works always, without fail.

Now, all my life I had been taught that where I sowed, there would I reap. But the real truth is, *what* I sow, I will reap. Not *where* I sow. I may not reap from the same place I sow. God may have me sow seeds in one person's field, and when harvest time comes, I may reap *from* the field of *someone else.* This is because the source of my harvesting is not the caretaker of the field—but God, who owns all.

What I make happen for others, God will make happen for me. That's the secret. That's the understanding that becomes your key to success. Don't look for your harvest *where* you have sowed. Look for your harvest *because* you have sowed.

Create success situations for others around you. Don't be surprised or alarmed if they fail to return the favor. You

---

Your Harvest Will Always Come Through The Door Of Someone In Trouble, Who Is Needing Your Help.

---

sow in the lives of others, but your *expectation of return is from* God, your heavenly Father, your *Source.*

So, the basic law is very simple. If you want to be a success—if you want to be fulfilled—concentrate on the success and fulfillment of others. Get your mind off yourself. Quit talking about your needs and your desires. Think of ways to create success for *the people around you.* Help *them* reach their goals. Help them become fulfilled and happy.

It *guarantees* your own success.

17

Creating a Zone of Success

What happens when you do this? When you make others successful, you create a "zone" of success. As you make the people around you successful, you are caught up in the middle of that success zone. And *what you have made happen for others, God will make happen for you.*

As I said earlier, this principle works both ways, for good or *bad*. Remember the story of Jacob in the Bible? He deceived his dying father to receive the blessing that should have been his brother's. But only a few years later, Jacob was deceived by his uncle, Laban. After working seven years to gain the hand of the fair Rachel in marriage, Jacob was given the older sister, Leah. He had to work seven more years for the girl he really wanted. What he made happen to someone else—deception—*happened to him.*

It also happens for *good*. Read I Kings 17:8-16 and you will find a fascinating success story. When a poor widow risked personal starvation in order to "create a success situation" for the prophet Elijah, God made that same miracle provision happen to her. *What she made happen for Elijah, God made happen for her!*

Though Job had experienced tremendous tragedies in his personal life, he got his mind off his own troubles and began to pray for his friends instead. Then his own miracle happened—the Lord turned his captivity! *"And the LORD turned the captivity of Job, when he prayed for his friends: also the LORD gave Job twice as much as he had before"* (Job 42:10).

Some time after God dealt with me so strongly on this subject, I was ministering in New Orleans, Louisiana. I urged the congregation to concentrate their efforts on making others successful, and God would make them successful. One young man really took my challenge to heart. He decided to put the principle to work with his boss.

He went to his employer and said, "I want to be your 'Success-Maker.' I want to make you more successful than you have ever been—the best boss you have ever been. I want you to make more money than you have ever made before. Just tell me what I can do to help you be more successful. Give me some of *your most difficult tasks* to do so you will be free to become more productive."

The young man's boss was completely shocked. He said, "No one has ever said that to me before. Tell me, why do you want to make me successful? What do *you* want out of it?"

The boy said, "I believe if I make you successful, then God will make me successful. If I help you to make more money for this business, then you will be able to pay me more. You'll be more successful, and so will I. I have wanted to make $6 an hour instead of $5. If I help you reach your goal, you will probably be able to help me achieve mine."

The boss said, "You will get your raise today. Anyone who cares about my success that much is surely worth $6 an hour!"

I believe with all my heart that this is one of the laws of God: *What you make happen for others, God will make happen for you.* Let this principle become part of the fabric of your Wisdom, and it will become a golden key in your hand to open every room of success you come to.

So start now. *Concentrate on the success of those around you.* How can you make your wife, your husband, your children more successful? How can you help your business or employer succeed in a greater way? What can you do to bless your church? Look for new ways to make everybody *around you* more successful. When you find such an opportunity, be quick to carry it out.

As you make them successful, God will bless you with success. *"Knowing that whatsoever good thing any man doeth, the same shall he receive of the Lord"* (Ephesians 6:8).

18

Where Do You Go From Here?

I have poured out my soul and a part of my very life to you in the pages of this book. I have shared in these pages what has taken me many years to learn. And it is my heartfelt prayer that God will use this book to inspire you and challenge you to find the success He has for you.

Let's take a moment to review the basic truths God anointed me to include:

1. **God wants you successful.** He wants your success to serve as an example of what He can do in a person's life. He wants you to succeed so you can provide for your family and be a strong spiritual leader for your loved ones. He wants your financial success to become a tool to help accomplish the great commission.

2. **The definition of success is achieving the goals God has for you as a person.** It is wanting what you get instead of getting what you want. It is not a destination, but the enjoyment experienced on the journey. It is finding fulfillment in every part of life—spiritual, physical, mental, financial, social and family.

3. **God's golden key to your success is—Wisdom.** Solomon could have asked for—and received—anything he wanted, including riches, power, or fame. But he chose the *master key* of Wisdom. As he used that key, he received all the other things as a bonus. What is Wisdom? It is learning to interpret life as God does—to see through His eyes, to hear through His ears, to comprehend with His mind. It is this ability that produces success in every area of your life.

4. **Wisdom is a gift only God can give.** He bestows it upon us through His Word. *So studying and feeding upon the Word produces Wisdom in us, and Wisdom produces success.*

5. **Developing a new picture of yourself is the way to begin moving into the realm of success.** Stop looking at the ugly, distorted, defeated picture of yourself which Satan would have you see. Instead, see yourself the way God sees you—full of potential and promise. See yourself in the image of God. What is God like? Exactly like His Son, Jesus, who was and is the supreme Success-Maker.

6. **Learn that what you make happen for others, God will make happen for you.** As you concentrate on putting good things into the lives of those around you, your own life will be filled with good things. As you create success for others, you find yourself living in a zone of success.

Having read these truths, where do you go from here? How can you apply them to your life to receive the most benefit?

Let me end this book with an admonition from the Word of God: *"This book of the law shall not depart out of thy mouth; but thou shalt meditate therein day and night, that thou mayest observe to do according to all that is written therein: for then thou shalt make thy way prosperous, and then thou shalt have good success"* (Joshua 1:8).

Remember. . .

God made you to *soar*. . .not sink!

God made you to *climb*. . .not crawl!

God made you to *fly*. . .not fall!

God made you to *stand*. . .not stumble!

May God bless you as you become more power conscious and live in the level of success He has designed just for you.

18

31 Facts About Wisdom

Your 31 Day Devotional

Fact 1
Wisdom Is The Master Key To All The Treasures Of Life.

"In that night did God appear unto Solomon, and said unto him, Ask what I shall give thee. And Solomon said unto God, Give me now wisdom and knowledge, And God said to Solomon, Because this was in thine heart, and thou hast not asked riches, wealth, or honour, nor the life of thine enemies, neither yet hast asked long life; Wisdom and knowledge is granted unto thee; and I will give thee riches, and wealth, and honour, such as none of the kings have had that have been before thee" (II Chronicles 1:7, 8a, 10a, 11a, 12a).

"In whom are hid all the treasures of wisdom and knowledge" (Colossians 2:3).

Fact 2
Wisdom Is A Gift From God To You.

"For the LORD giveth wisdom: out of his mouth cometh knowledge and understanding" (Proverbs 2:6).

"For to one is given by the Spirit the word of wisdom; to another the word of knowledge by the same Spirit" (I Corinthians 12:8).

"And came and preached peace to you which were afar off, and to them that were nigh" (Ephesians 2:17).

"He giveth wisdom unto the wise, and knowledge to them that know understanding" (Daniel 2:21b).

"Talk no more so exceeding proudly; let not arrogancy come out of your mouth: for the LORD is a God of knowledge, and by him actions are weighed" (I Samuel 2:3).

Fact 3
The Fear Of God Is The Beginning Of Wisdom.

"The fear of the LORD is the beginning of wisdom: and the knowledge of the holy is understanding" (Proverbs 9:10).

"The fear of the LORD is the beginning of wisdom: a good understanding have all they that do his commandments: his praise endureth for ever". (Psalms 111:10).

"And unto man he said, Behold, the fear of the Lord, that is wisdom; and to depart from evil is understanding" (Job 28:28).

Fact 4
The Wisdom Of The World Is A False Substitute For The Wisdom Of God.

"And my speech and my preaching was not with entic-ing words of man's wisdom, but in demonstration of the Spirit and of power." Which things also we speak, not in the words which man's wisdom teacheth, but which the Holy Ghost teacheth; comparing spiritual things with spiritual" (I Corinthians 2:4,13).

"Who is a wise man and endued with knowledge among you? let him shew out of a good conversation his works with meekness of wisdom. But if ye have bitter envy-ing and strife in your hearts, glory not, and lie not against the truth. This wisdom descendeth not from above, but is earthly, sensual, devilish. For where envying and strife is, there is confusion and every evil work. But the wisdom that is from above is first pure, then peaceable, gentle, and easy to be entreated, full of mercy and good fruits, without partiality, and without hypocrisy" (James 3:13-17).

Fact 5
The Wisdom Of Man Is Foolishness To God.

"Where is the wise? where is the scribe? where is the dis-puter of this world? hath not God made foolish the wisdom of this world? For after that in the wisdom of God the world by wisdom knew not God, it pleased God by the fool-ishness of preaching to save them that believe. Because the

foolishness of God is wiser than men; and the weakness of God is stronger than men" (I Corinthians 1:20-21,25).

"For the wisdom of this world is foolishness with God. For it is written, He taketh the wise in their own craftiness" (I Corinthians 3:19).

Fact 6
Right Relationships Increase Your Wisdom.

"He that walketh with wise men shall be wise: but a companion of fools shall be destroyed" (Proverbs 13:20).

"Be not deceived: evil communications corrupt good manners" (I Corinthians 15:33).

"Now we command you, brethren, in the name of our Lord Jesus Christ, that ye withdraw yourselves from every brother that walketh disorderly, and not after the tradition which he received of us" (II Thessalonians 3:6).

"Perverse disputings of men of corrupt minds, and destitute of the truth, supposing that gain is godliness: from such withdraw thyself" (I Timothy 6:5).

Fact 7
The Wisdom Of God Is Foolishness To The Natural Mind.

"And my speech and my preaching was not with enticing words of man's wisdom, but in demonstration of

the Spirit and of power. That your faith should not stand in the wisdom of men, but in the power of God" (I Corinthians 2:4-5).

"A fool hath no delight in understanding" (Proverbs 18:2).

"For my thoughts are not your thoughts, neither are your ways my ways, saith the LORD. For as the heavens are higher than the earth, so are my ways higher than your ways, and my thoughts than your thoughts" (Isaiah 55:8-9).

Fact 8
Your Conversation Reveals How Much Wisdom You Possess.

"And all the earth sought to Solomon, to hear his wisdom, which God had put in his heart" (I Kings 10:24).

"A fool uttereth all his mind: but a wise man keepeth it in till afterwards" (Proverbs 29:11).

"Death and life are in the power of the tongue: and they that love it shall eat the fruit thereof" (Proverbs 18:21).

"For in many things we offend all. If any man offend not in word, the same is a perfect man, and able also to bridle the whole body" (James 3:2).

Fact 9
Jesus Is Made Unto Us Wisdom.

"But of him are ye in Christ Jesus, who of God is made unto us wisdom, and righteousness, and sanctification, and redemption" (I Corinthians 1:30).

"Having predestinated us unto the adoption of children by Jesus Christ to himself, according to the good pleasure of his will, Wherein he hath abounded toward us in all wisdom and prudence; That the God of our Lord Jesus Christ, the Father of glory, may give unto you the spirit of wisdom and revelation in the knowledge of him" (Ephesians 1:5,8,17).

Fact 10
All The Treasures Of Wisdom And Knowledge Are Hid In Jesus Christ.

"That their hearts might be comforted, being knit together in love, and unto all riches of the full assurance of understanding, to the acknowledgment of the mystery of God, and of the Father, and of Christ; In whom are hid all the treasures of wisdom and knowledge" (Colossians 2:2-3).

"But we preach Christ crucified, unto the Jews a stumblingblock, and unto the Greeks foolishness; But unto them which are called, both Jews and Greeks, Christ the power of God, and the wisdom of God" (I Corinthians 1:23-24).

"But we speak the wisdom of God in a mystery, even the hidden wisdom, which God ordained before the world

unto our glory. Which none of the princes of this world knew: for had they known it, they would not have cruci- fied the Lord of glory" (I Corinthians 2:7-8).

Fact 11
The Word Of God Is Your Source Of Wisdom.

"Behold, I have taught you statutes and judgments, even as the LORD my God commanded me, that ye should do so in the land whither ye go to possess it. . . . For this is your wisdom and your understanding in the sight of the nations" (Deuteronomy 4:5-6a).

"Thou through thy commandments hast made me wiser than mine enemies: for they are ever with me. I have more understanding than all my teachers: for thy testimonies are my meditation. I understand more than the ancients, because I keep thy precepts" .
(Psalms 119:98-100).

"For the LORD giveth wisdom: out of his mouth cometh knowledge and understanding" (Proverbs 2:6).

Fact 12
God Will Give You Wisdom When You Take The Time To Listen.

"For the LORD giveth wisdom: out of his mouth cometh knowledge and understanding" (Proverbs 2:6).

"My sheep hear my voice, and I know them, and they follow me:" (John 10:27).

"If any of you lack wisdom, let him ask of God, that giveth to all men liberally, and upbraideth not; and it shall be given him" (James 1:5).

"But they that wait upon the LORD shall renew their strength; they shall mount up with wings as eagles; they shall run, and not be weary; and they shall walk, and not faint" (Isaiah 40:31).

Fact 13
The Word Of God Is Able To Make You Wise Unto Salvation.

"And that from a child thou hast known the holy scriptures, which are able to make thee wise unto salvation through faith which is in Christ Jesus" (II Timothy 3:15).

"Whoso is wise, and will observe these things, even they shall understand the lovingkindness of the LORD" (Psalms 107:43).

"Search the scriptures; for in them ye think ye have eternal life: and they are they which testify of me" (John 5:39).

Fact 14
The Holy Spirit Is The Spirit Of Wisdom That Unleashes Your Gifts, Talents And Skills.

"And the LORD spake unto Moses, saying, And I have filled him with the spirit of God, in wisdom, and in under-

standing, and in knowledge, and in all manner of work-manship, To devise cunning works, to work in gold, and in silver, and in brass" (Exodus 31:1,3-4).

"In whom the LORD put wisdom and understanding to know how to work all manner of work for the service of the sanctuary, according to all that the LORD had com-manded" (Exodus 36:1).

"Children in whom was no blemish, but well favoured, and skilful in all wisdom, and cunning in knowledge, and understanding science, and such as had ability in them to stand in the king's palace, and whom they might teach the learning and the tongue of the Chaldeans" (Daniel 1:4).

Fact 15
Men Of Wisdom Will Always Be Men Of Mercy.

"But the wisdom that is from above is first pure, then peaceable, gentle, and easy to be intreated, full of mercy and good fruits, without partiality, and without hypocrisy" (James 3:17).

"Brethren, if any of you do err from the truth, and one convert him; Let him know, that he which converteth the sinner from the error of his way shall save a soul from death, and shall hide a multitude of sins" (James 5:19-20).

"Brethren, if a man be overtaken in a fault, ye which are spiritual, restore such an one in the spirit of meekness; considering thyself, lest thou also be tempted. Bear ye one

another's burdens, and so fulfil the law of Christ" (Galatians 6:1-2).

Fact 16
Wisdom Is Better Than Jewels Or Money.

"For wisdom is better than rubies; and all the things that may be desired are not to be compared to it" *(Proverbs 8:11).*

"Happy is the man that findeth wisdom, and the man that getteth understanding. For the merchandise of it is better than the merchandise of silver, and the gain thereof than fine gold. She is more precious than rubies: and all the things thou canst desire are not to be compared unto her" (Proverbs 3:13-15).

"For the price of wisdom is above rubies" (Job 28:18b).

"How much better is it to get wisdom than gold! and to get understanding rather to be chosen than silver!" (Proverbs 16:16).

Fact 17
Wisdom Is More Powerful Than Weapons Of War.

"Wisdom is better than weapons of war: but one sinner destroyeth much good" (Ecclesiastes 9:18).

"And wisdom and knowledge shall be the stability of thy times, and strength of salvation: the fear of the LORD is his treasure" (Isaiah 33:6).

"But the mouth of the upright shall deliver them" (Proverbs 12:6b).

"And they were not able to resist the wisdom and the spirit by which he spake" (Acts 6:10).

Fact 18
The Mantle Of Wisdom Makes You Ten Times Stronger Than Those Without It.

"Wisdom strengtheneth the wise more than ten mighty men which are in the city" (Ecclesiastes 7:19).

"As for these four children, God gave them knowledge and skill in all learning and wisdom: and Daniel had understanding in all visions and dreams. And in all matters of wisdom and understanding, that the king inquired of them, he found them ten times better than all the magicians and astrologers that were in all his realm" (Daniel 1:17,20).

"A thousand shall fall at thy side, and ten thousand at thy right hand; but it shall not come nigh thee" (Psalms 91:7).

Fact 19
The Wise Hate Evil And The Evil Hate The Wise.

"The fear of the LORD is to hate evil: pride, and arrogancy, and the evil way, and the froward mouth, do I hate" (Proverbs 8:13).

"The fear of the LORD is the beginning of knowledge: but fools despise wisdom and instruction" (Proverbs 1:7).

"Reprove not a scorner, lest he hate thee: rebuke a wise man, and he will love thee" (Proverbs 9:8).

A fool hath no delight in understanding" (Proverbs 18:2).

"How long, ye simple ones, will ye love simplicity? and the scorners delight in their scorning, and fools hate knowledge?" (Proverbs 1:22).

Fact 20
Wisdom Reveals The Treasure In Yourself.

"He that getteth wisdom loveth his own soul: he that keepeth understanding shall find good" (Proverbs 19:8).

"Being confident of this very thing, that he which hath begun a good work in you will perform it until the day of Jesus Christ" (Philippians 1:6).

"But ye are a chosen generation, a royal priesthood, an holy nation, a peculiar people; that ye should show forth the praises of him who hath called you out of darkness into his marvellous light: Which in time past were not a people, but are now the people of God: which had not obtained mercy, but now have obtained mercy" (I Peter 2:9-10).

"For we are his workmanship, created in Christ Jesus unto good works, which God hath before ordained that we should walk in them" (Ephesians 2:10).

Fact 21
The Proof Of Wisdom Is The Presence Of Joy And Peace.

"For wisdom is a defence, and money is a defence: but the excellency of knowledge is, that wisdom giveth life to them that have it" (Ecclesiastes 7:12).

"Happy is the man that findeth wisdom, and the man that getteth understanding" (Proverbs 3:13).

"But the wisdom that is from above is first pure, then peaceable, gentle, and easy to be entreated, full of mercy and good fruits, without partiality, and without hypocrisy" (James 3:17).

"Great peace have they which love thy law: and nothing shall offend them" (Psalms 119:165).

Fact 22
Wisdom Makes Your Enemies Helpless Against You.

"For I will give you a mouth and wisdom, which all your adversaries shall not be able to gainsay nor resist" (Luke 21:15).

"When a man's ways please the LORD, he maketh even his enemies to be at peace with him" (Proverbs 16:7).

"No weapon that is formed against thee shall prosper; and every tongue that shall rise against thee in judgment thou shalt condemn. This is the heritage of the servants of the LORD, and their righteousness is of me, saith the LORD" (Isaiah 54:17).

"For wisdom is a defence, and money is a defence: but the excellency of knowledge is, that wisdom giveth life to them that have it" (Ecclesiastes 7:12).

"For the LORD giveth wisdom: To deliver thee from the way of the evil man, To deliver thee from the strange woman" (Proverbs 2:6a, 12a, 16a).

Fact 23
Wisdom Creates Currents Of Favor And Recognition Toward You.

"Exalt her, and she shall promote thee: she shall bring thee to honour, when thou dost embrace her" (Proverbs 4:8).

"Blessed is the man that heareth me, watching daily at my gates, waiting at the posts of my doors. For whoso findeth me findeth life, and shall obtain favour of the LORD" (Proverbs 8:34-35).

"My son, forget not my law; So shalt thou find favour and good understanding in the sight of God and man" (Proverbs 3:1a, 4).

Fact 24
The Wise Welcome Correction.

"Reprove not a scorner, lest he hate thee: rebuke a wise man, and he will love thee. Give instruction to a wise man, and he will be yet wiser: teach a just man, and he will increase in learning" (Proverbs 9:8-9).

"The ear that heareth the reproof of life abideth among the wise. He that refuseth instruction despiseth his own soul: but he that heareth reproof getteth understanding" (Proverbs 15:31-32).

"My son, despise not the chastening of the LORD; neither be weary of his correction: For whom the LORD loveth he correcteth; even as a father the son in whom he delighteth" (Proverbs 3:11-12).

Fact 25
When The Wise Speak, Healing Flows.

"There is that speaketh like the piercings of a sword: but the tongue of the wise is health" (Proverbs 12:18).

"The tongue of the wise useth knowledge aright: but the mouth of fools poureth out foolishness. A wholesome

tongue is a tree of life: but perverseness therein is a breach in the spirit" (Proverbs 15:2, 4).

"The tongue of the just is as choice silver: The lips of the righteous feed many" (Proverbs 10:20a, 21a).

"Death and life are in the power of the tongue: and they that love it shall eat the fruit thereof" (Proverbs 18:21).

"The mouth of a righteous man is a well of life: but violence covereth the mouth of the wicked" (Proverbs 10:11).

Fact 26
When You Increase Your Wisdom You Will Increase Your Wealth.

"Riches and honour are with me; yea, durable riches and righteousness. That I may cause those that love me to inherit substance; and I will fill their treasures (Proverbs 8:18,21).

"Length of days is in her right hand; and in her left hand riches and honour" (Proverbs 3:16).

"Blessed is the man that feareth the LORD, that delighteth greatly in his commandments. Wealth and riches shall be in his house" (Psalms 112:1b, 3a).

"The crown of the wise is their riches" (Proverbs 14:24).

Fact 27
Wisdom Can Be Imparted By The Laying On Of Hands Of A Man Of God.

"Wherefore I put thee in remembrance that thou stir up the gift of God, which is in thee by the putting on of my hands. That good thing which was committed unto thee keep by the Holy Ghost which dwelleth in us" (II Timothy 1:6, 14).

"And Joshua the son of Nun was full of the spirit of wisdom" (Deuteronomy 34:9).

"Whom they set before the apostles: and when they had prayed, they laid their hands on them. And Stephen, full of faith and power, did great wonders and miracles among the people. And they were not able to resist the wisdom and the spirit by which he spake" (Acts 6:6, 8, 10).

Fact 28
Wisdom Guarantees Promotion.

"By me kings reign, and princes decree justice. By me princes rule, and nobles, even all the judges of the earth" (Proverbs 8:15-16).

"And thou, Ezra, after the wisdom of thy God, that is in thine hand, set magistrates and judges, which may judge all the people that are beyond the river, all such as know the laws of thy God; and teach ye them that know them not" (Ezra 7:25).

"Exalt her, and she shall promote thee: she shall bring thee to honour, when thou dost embrace her. She shall give to thine head an ornament of grace: a crown of glory shall she deliver to thee" (Proverbs 4:8-9).

Fact 29
Wisdom Loves Those Who Love Her.

"I love them that love me; and those that seek me early shall find me" (Proverbs 8:17).

"That I may cause those that love me to inherit substance; and I will fill their treasures" (Proverbs 8:21).

"Yea, if thou criest after knowledge, and liftest up thy voice for understanding; If thou seekest her as silver, and searchest for her as for hid treasures; Then shalt thou understand the fear of the LORD, and find the knowledge of God" (Proverbs 2:3-5).

Fact 30
Wisdom Will Be Given To You When You Pray For It In Faith.

"If any of you lack wisdom, let him ask of God, that giveth to all men liberally, and upbraideth not; and it shall be given him. But let him ask in faith, nothing wavering" (James 1:5-6a).

"Ask, and it shall be given you; seek, and ye shall find; knock, and it shall be opened unto you: For every one that asketh receiveth; and he that seeketh findeth; and to him

that knocketh it shall be opened. If ye then, being evil, know how to give good gifts unto your children, how much more shall your Father which is in heaven give good things to them that ask him?" (Matthew 7:7-8,11).

Fact 31
He That Wins Souls Is Wise.

"The fruit of the righteous is a tree of life; and he that winneth souls is wise" (Proverbs 11:30).

"And they that be wise shall shine as the brightness of the firmament; and they that turn many to righteousness as the stars for ever and ever" (Daniel 12:3).

"How then shall they call on him in whom they have not believed? and how shall they believe in him of whom they have not heard? and how shall they hear without a preacher? And how shall they preach, except they be sent? as it is written, How beautiful are the feet of them that preach the gospel of peace, and bring glad tidings of good things!" (Romans 10:14-15).

ABOUT MIKE MURDOCK

► Has embraced his assignment to pursue...possess...and publish the Wisdom of God to heal the broken in his generation.

► Preached his first public sermon at the age of 8.

► Preached his first evangelistic crusade at the age of 15.

► Began full-time evangelism at the age of 19, in which he has continued for 28 years.

► Has traveled and spoken to more than 11,000 audiences in 36 countries, including East Africa, the Orient, and Europe.

► Receives more than 1,500 invitation each year to speak in churches, colleges, and business corporations.

► Noted author of 57 books, including the best sellers, "Wisdom for Winning", "Dream-Seeds", and "The Double Diamond Principle".

► Created the popular "Wisdom Topical Bible" series for Businessmen, Mothers, Fathers, Teenagers, and the One-Minute Pocket Bible.

► Has composed more than 1,200 songs such as "I Am Blessed", "You Can Make It", and "Jesus Just The Mention of Your Name", recorded by many gospel artists.

► He has released over 20 music albums as well, and the music video, "Going Back To The Word".

► Is a dynamic teacher having produced to date 21 Wisdom Teaching Tape series and 9 School of Wisdom videos.

► He has appeared often on TBN, CBN, and other television network programs.

► Is a Founding Trustee on the Board of Charismatic Bible Ministries.

► Is the Founder of the Wisdom Training Center, for the training of those entering the ministry.

► Has had more than 3,400 accept the call into full-time ministry under his ministry.

► Has a goal of establishing Wisdom Rooms in one million Christian homes.

► Has a weekly television program called "Wisdom for Crisis Times".

MY DECISION PAGE

May I Invite You To Make Jesus The Lord of Your Life?

The Bible says, "that if thou shalt confess with thy mouth the Lord Jesus Christ, and shalt believe in thine heart that God hath raised him from the dead, thou shalt be saved. For with the heart man believeth unto righteousness; and with the mouth confession is made unto salvation." (Romans 10:9,10)

To receive Jesus Christ as Lord and Saviour of your life, please pray this prayer from your heart today!

Dear Jesus,

I believe that You died for me and that You arose again on the third day. I confess to You that I am a sinner and that I need Your love and forgiveness. Come into my life, forgive my sins, and give me eternal life. I confess You now as my Saviour! I walk in your peace and joy from this day forward.

Signed _____

Date _____

☐ Yes, Mike, I have accepted Christ as my personal Saviour and would like to receive my personal gift copy of your book *31 Keys To A New Beginning.* (B 48) #DC10

Name _____

Address _____

City _____ State _____ Zip _____

Phone ( )_____ Birthdate _____

Occupation _____

YOUR LETTER IS VERY IMPORTANT TO ME

You are a special person to me, and I believe you are special to God. I want to help you in every way I can. Let me hear from you when you are facing spiritual needs or experiencing a conflict in your life, or if you just want to know that someone really cares. Write me. I will pray for your needs. And I will write you back something that I know will help you receive the miracle you need.

Mike, here are my special needs at this time:
-Please Print-

_____

_____

_____

_____

_____

_____

_____

_____

_____

_____

_____

_____

Mail To:

MIKE MURDOCK

The Wisdom Center • P.O. Box 99 • Dallas, Texas 75221

CLIP & MAIL

WILL YOU BECOME A WISDOM KEY PARTNER?

1. TELEVISION - The Way Of The Winner, a nationally-syndicated weekly TV program features Mike Murdock's teaching and music.

2. WTC - Wisdom Training Center where Dr. Murdock trains those preparing for full-time ministry in a special 70 Hour Training Program.

3. MISSIONS - Recent overseas outreaches include crusades to East Africa, Brazil and Poland; 1,000 Young Minister's Handbooks sent to India to train nationals for ministry to their people..

4. MUSIC - Millions of people have been blessed by the anointed song-writing and singing talents of Mike Murdock, who has recorded over 20 highly-acclaimed albums.

5. LITERATURE - Best-selling books, teaching tapes and magazines proclaim the Wisdom of God.

6. CRUSADES - Multitudes are ministered to in crusades and seminars throughout America as Mike Murdock declares life-giving principles from God's Word.

7. SCHOOLS OF WISDOM - Each year Mike Murdock hosts Schools of Wisdom for those who want personalized and advanced training for achieving their dreams and goals.

I want to personally invite you to be a part of this ministry!

CLIP & MAIL

Wisdom Key Partnership Plan

Dear Partner,

God has brought us together! I love representing you as I spread His Wisdom in the world. Will you become my Faith-Partner? Your Seed is powerful. When you sow, three benefits are guaranteed: PROTECTION (Mal. 3:10-11), FAVOR (Luke 6:38), FINANCIAL PROSPERITY (Deut. 8:18). Please note the four levels as a monthly Wisdom Key Faith Partner. Complete the response sheet and rush it to me immediately. Then focus your expectations for the 100-fold return (Mark 10:30)!

Your Faith Partner,

Mike Murdock

Yes, Mike, I want to be a Wisdom Key Partner with you. Please rush The Wisdom Key Partnership Pak to me today!

- ❑ **Foundation Partner...**Yes, Mike, I want to be a Wisdom Key Foundation Partner. Enclosed is my first monthly Seed-Faith Promise of $15.
- ❑ **Seed-a-Day...**Yes, Mike, I want to be a Wisdom Key Partner as a Seed-a-Day member. Enclosed is my first monthly Seed-Faith Promise of $30.
- ❑ **Covenant of Blessing...**Yes, Mike, I want to be a Wisdom Key Partner as a Covenant of Blessing member. Enclosed is my first Seed-Faith Promise of $58.
- ❑ **The Seventy...**Yes, Mike, I want to be a Wisdom Key Partner as a member of The Seventy. Enclosed is my first monthly Seed-Faith Promise of $100.

TOTAL ENCLOSED $ ______ #DC10

Name ____

Address ____

City ________________ State ________ Zip ____________

Phone ( ) __________________ Birthday ______________

Mail To:

MIKE MURDOCK

The Wisdom Center • P.O. Box 99 • Dallas, Texas 75221

WISDOM KEY PARTNERSHIP PAK

W hen you become a Wisdom Key Monthly Faith Partner or a part of The Seventy, you will receive our Partnership Pak which includes:

1. *Special Music Cassette*
2. *101 Wisdom Keys Book*
3. *Partnership Coupon Book*

Yes Mike! I Want To Be Your Partner!

❏ Enclosed is my best Seed-Faith Gift of $_____.

❏ I want to be a Wisdom Key Partner! Enclosed is my first Seed-Faith gift of $_____ for the first month.

❏ Please rush my special Partnership Pak. (#PP02)

Name _____

Address _____

City _____State _____Zip _____

Phone (   )_____

#DC10

Mail To:

MIKE MURDOCK

The Wisdom Center • P.O. Box 99 • Dallas, Texas 75221

4 POWER-PACKED TAPE SERIES BY MIKE MURDOCK

HOW TO WALK THROUGH FIRE

The 4 basic causes of conflict and how to react in a personal crisis, which are extremely helpful for those who are walking through the fires of marriage difficulty, divorce, depression, and financial adversity. (TS5) Six Tape Series

$30

THE ASSIGNMENT

Do you wonder why you are here? What are you to do? These tapes will unlock the hidden treasures inside you to fulfill the *Assignment* God has called you to. 160 Wisdom Keys that can reveal the purpose of God. (TS22) Six Tape Series

$30

WOMEN THAT MEN CANNOT FORGET

Discover the success secrets of two of the most remarkable women in history...and how their secrets can help you achieve your dreams and goals! Both men and women will enjoy these wisdom secrets from the lives of Ruth and Esther. (TS31)Six Tape Series

$30

THE GRASSHOPPER COMPLEX

A must for those who need more self-confidence! It reveals the secrets of overcoming every giant you face in achieving your personal dreams and goals. (TS3)Six Tape Series

$30

Order All Four Series & Pay Only $100

6 Wisdom Books

WISDOM FOR CRISIS TIMES

Discover the Wisdom Keys to dealing with tragedies, stress and times of crisis. Secrets that will unlock the questions in the right way to react in life situations. (Paperback)

(BK08) 118 Pages.....$7

SEEDS OF WISDOM

One-Year Daily Devotional. A 374 page devotional with topics on dreams and goals, relationships, miracles, prosperity and more! (Paperback)

(BK02) 374 Pages.....$10

ONE-YEAR TOPICAL BIBLE

A One-Minute reference Bible. 365 topics; spiritual, topical and easy to read. A collection of Scriptures relating to specific topics that challenge and concern you. (Paperback)

(BK03) 374 Pages.....$10

THE DOUBLE DIAMOND PRINCIPLE

58 Master Secrets For Total Success, in the life of Jesus that will help you achieve your dreams and goals. (Paperback)

(BK71) 118 Pages.....$7

WISDOM FOR WINNING

The best-selling handbook for achieving success. If you desire to be successful and happy, this is the book for you! (Paperback)

(BK23) 280 Pages.....$9

DREAM SEEDS

What do you dream of doing with you life? What would you attempt to do if you knew it was impossible to fail? This 118-page book helps you answer these questions and much more! (Paperback)

(BK20) 118 Pages.....$7

ORDER FORM

Item No.	Name of Item	Quantity	Price Per Item	Total
#TS22	The Assignment Tapes		30.00	$
#TS5	How To Walk Through Fire Tapes		30.00	$
#TS3	The Grasshopper Complex Tapes		30.00	$
#TS3	Women Men Cannot Forget Tapes		30.00	$
	All 4 Tape Series For $100.00			$
#BK20	Dream Seeds Book		7.00	$
#BK23	Wisdom For Winning Book		9.00	$
#BK20	Seeds of Wisdom Book (374 Pgs)		10.00	$
#BK71	Double Diamond Principle Book		7.00	$
#BK08	Wisdom For Crisis Times Book		7.00	$
#BK03	One Minute Topical Bible (374 Pgs)		10.00	$
SORRY NO C.O.D's	Add 10% For Shipping			$
	(Canada add 20%)			$
	Enclosed is my Seed-Faith Gift for Your Ministry.			$
#DC10	Total Amount Enclosed			$

Please Print

Name

Address

City

State   Zip

Phone(hm)   (wk)

☐ Check   ☐ Money Order   ☐ Cash

☐ Visa   ☐ MasterCard   ☐ AMEX

Signature_____

Card#

Expiration Date _____

☐ Send Free Catalog & Free Subscription To Newsletter *Wisdom Talk*

Mail To:

MIKE MURDOCK

The Wisdom Center • P.O. Box 99 • Dallas, Texas 75221

CLIP & MAIL